COWGIRLS

COWGIRLS

STRONG · SAVVY · SPIRITED

WILLOW CREEK PRESS

Published by Willow Creek Press
P.O. Box 147
Minocqua, Wisconsin 54548

Photo Credits; p2 © Londie G. Padelsky; p5,7 © Robert Dawson; p8 © Londie G. Padelsky; p11,12 © J.C. Leacock; p 15 © Eric Berndt/The Image Finders; p16 © Londie G. Padelsky; p19 © Ron Kimball/ronkimballstock.com; p20 © Robert Dawson; p23 © J.C. Leacock; p24 © Mark S. Werner/The Image Finders; p27 © J.C. Leacock; p28 © Robert Dawson; p31© J.C. Leacock; p32 © Ron Kimball/ronkimballstock.com; p35,36,39 © J.C. Leacock; p40 © Mark S. Werner/The Image Finders; p43,44,47,48 © J.C. Leacock; p51 © Robert Dawson; p52,56 © J.C. Leacock; p57,59,60 © Robert Dawson; p63 © J.C. Leacock; p64 © Robert Dawson; p67 © Mark Gibson/The Image Finders; p68 © Robert Dawson; p71 © J.C. Leacock; p72 © Robert Dawson; p75 J.C. Leacock; p76 © Robert Dawson; p79 © J.C. Leacock; p80 © Robert Dawson; p83 © J.C. Leacock; p84 © Londie G. Padelsky; p87 © Ron Kimball/ronkimballstock.com; p88 © Mark S. Werner; p91 © Londie G. Padelsky; p92,95,96 © J.C. Leacock;

Design: Donnie Rubo
Printed in Canada

Cowgirl: A better-looking cowboy with brains.

Toughness doesn't have to
come in a pinstriped suit.

Dianne Feinstein

To tell a woman everything she may not do is to tell her what she can do.

Spanish Proverb

If the world was truly a rational place,
men would ride sidesaddle.

Rita Mae Brown

A cowgirl would no more think of wearing spike heels, a tight girdle, a binding brassiere, than she would drink poison. It's not that a cowgirl does not want to attract the masculine eyes, but we know cowboys. They like slimness, line, grace—but they want it natural.

Alice Greenough

Heels and pointed toes cramp your viewpoint.

Alice Greenough

He learned to wrangle horses and to try to know them all, and get them in at daylight if he could, or. . . was it she?

Little Joe the Wrangler

I'd rather be dumped by a horse
than dumped by a man!

———⊰•⊱———

My horse don't care about the wrinkles.
He knows who I am, anyway.

Frances Bentley

Taking joy in life is a woman's best cosmetic.

Rosalind Russell

She'll match the wits of any man
No matter what he might say
Then out-work that sorry cuss
In kitchen, corral, or buckin' hay!

If ya' done it, it ain't braggin'.

Old Texas saying

With chaps and hat and rope in hand
She can do anything any cowboy can!

The Cowgirl Waltz

Ride? Why, she can cut a critter
From the herd as neat as pie,
Read a brand out on the ranges
Just as well as you or I.

Our Little Cowgirl

If you want anything said, ask a man.
If you want something done, ask a women.

Margaret Thatcher

The things that you do in barrel racing are the same things that you do in life when you really want to succeed: you're motivated, you're organized; you're a good image; you're setting goals, and you're always looking for ways to do it better.

Martha Josey

Let's put it this way, you can criticize me, my husband and even the children. But don't ever criticize my horses.

Ann Lowdon Call

When your ship comes in, it just might be a horse.

Jan Jasion Cross

When riding my horse I no longer have my heart in my chest, but between my knees.

There's such rhythm with riding—not just the rhythm of the beat of the horse's hooves, but the rhythm of the blood surging between you.

Chris Hawkins

If you've never been thrown you never rode.

L.D. Burke

There is no other source of energy that
revitalizes me as much as being with a horse.

Jill Hassler

In riding a horse we borrow freedom.

Helen Thomson

There's a solitude and a refreshing connection with nature that you can't get in a city with other people around. We need to realize that we're not above nature, we're simply a part of it.

Bev Doolittle

I saw her ride the Arroyo,
   back on the Idaho sands,
She smiled like an acre of sunflowers
   with her quirt in her hand.

The Santa Fe Trail

Somewhere it's said she still spurs the high range
With a posse of maidens on wild mustangs.

The Ballad of the Belle Star

I'm just like these old oak trees. I'm rooted in here so deep there's just no movin' me.

Mildred Kauipe

I have any number of troubles, in fact too numerous to mention, but I forget them all in this joyous air with the grand protecting mountains always standing round the western horizon.

Mary E. Inderwich

Sell the cow, buy the sheep,
but never be without the horse.

Irish proverb

I have any number of troubles, in fact too numerous to mention, but I forget them all in this joyous air with the grand protecting mountains always standing round the western horizon.

Mary E. Inderwich

Sell the cow, buy the sheep,
but never be without the horse.

Irish proverb

A horse is worth more than rides.

Spanish proverb

**A pony is a childhood dream,
a horse is an adulthood treasure.**

Rebecca Carroll

Everything depends upon
myself and my horse.

Mamie Francis

It's so easy to train horses; it's almost
impossible to train the owners.

Glenn Randall

Horses are a direct reflection of the people that handle them.

John Lyons

You gotta mean what you say and say what you mean to horses. Without total integrity, there's no hope of ever forging a bond with any horse.

Macella O'Neill

If you learn anything from horses, the very
first thing is the give and take of love.

Ron Harding

To be loved by a horse should fill us with
awe—for we have not deserved it.

Marion C. Garrett

Horses are individual beings—as humans are.

Mary Fenton

The essential joy of being with horses is that it brings us in contact with the rare elements of grace, beauty, spirit, and fire.

Sharon Ralls Lemon

Horses challenge humans to get out of
their heads more and to listen to their
instincts, feelings, and intuitions.

Diana Thompson

A horse can lend its rider the speed and strength he or she lacks, but the rider who is wise remembers it is no more than a loan.

Pam Brown

With the new day comes new strength and new thoughts.

Eleanor Roosevelt

Do not follow where the path may lead, go instead where there is no path and leave a trail.

All leaders are born from women.

If we cannot find the road
to success, we will make one.

Cowgirl's Motto